# ISAA LEARNS ISLAM

## Beginning with Bismillah

Written by Ali Mansoor
Illustrated by Abeer Kasiri

Join Isaa On All His Adventures! More Details at
www.kidslearnislam.com

Dedicated to all mothers,
everywhere.

Once upon a time,
In a land not far away.
Lived a boy named Isaa,
Who sure loved to play!

Early one morning,
Before the sun began to shine.
Barely awake, he began shouting,
"It's play time! It's play time!"

In his haste.
He stepped on a toy.
Tears in his eyes,
Gone was the joy.

Finishing her prayers,
Across the hall.
Mommy knew what happened,
She heard Isaa bawl.

Holding Isaa close,
Safe in her arms.
She gave him advice,
And a hug so warm.

"My lovely little Isaa,
You're so eager to play.
Before starting anything,
Remember to say.

BIS-MIL-LAH

When you wake up every morning.
After you're done stretching and yawning.
Before starting your day.
Always remember to say.

BIS-MIL-LAH

When sitting at the table.
As soon as you're able.
Before your first bite.
Don't forget to recite

# BIS-MIL-LAH

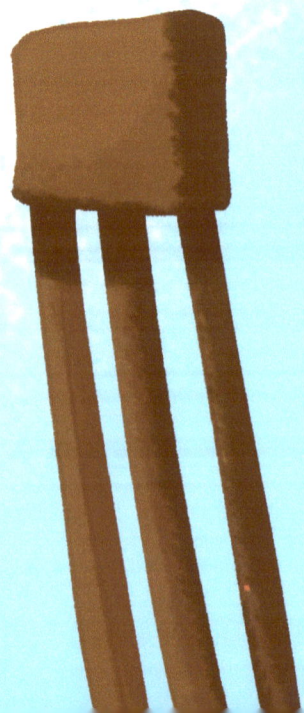

Before jumping rope,
Or riding a bike.
Say a quick word,
To start things right.

WHISPER
BIS-MIL-LAH

If beginning a race.
Don't think about your pace.
With His name you begin.
For sure you will win!

START WITH

BIS-MIL-LAH!

Before coming inside,
Or when stepping out.
One word to remember,
No need to shout.

BIS-MIL-LAH

Isaa jumped with excitement,
For now he knew.
Before starting a task,
what he had to do.

He would pause,
He would close his eyes.
In His name we begin,
He is merciful and wise.

SAY BIS-MIL-LAH!

Join Isaa On All His Adventures!
More Details at

www.kidslearnislam.com

www.ingramcontent.com/pod-product-compliance
Lightning Source LLC
Chambersburg PA
CBHW042110040426
42448CB00002B/216